CW01640764

by Iain Gray

LangSyne
PUBLISHING
WRITING *to* REMEMBER

LangSyne
PUBLISHING
WRITING *to* REMEMBER

79 Main Street, Newtongrange,
Midlothian EH22 4NA
Tel: 0131 344 0414 Fax: 0845 075 6085
E-mail: info@lang-syne.co.uk
www.langsyneshop.co.uk

Design by Dorothy Meikle
Printed by Printwell Ltd

ISBN 978-1-85217-605-1

Wood

MOTTOES include:
The tree may be recognised by its fruits
(and)
Defend.

CRESTS include:
An oak tree
(and)
A demi-savage wielding a club.

NAME variations include:
Woods

Chapter one:

The origins of popular surnames

by George Forbes and Iain Gray

If you don't know where you came from, you won't know where you're going **is a frequently quoted observation and one that has a particular resonance today when there has been a marked upsurge in interest in genealogy, with increasing numbers of people curious to trace their family roots.**

Main sources for genealogical research include census returns and official records of births, marriages and deaths – and the key to unlocking the detail they contain is obviously a family surname, one that has been 'inherited' and passed from generation to generation.

No matter our station in life, we all have a surname – but it was not until about the middle of the fourteenth century that the practice of being identified by a particular surname became commonly established throughout the British Isles.

Previous to this, it was normal for a person to be identified through the use of only a forename.

But as population gradually increased and there were many more people with the same forename, surnames were adopted to distinguish one person, or community, from another.

Many common English surnames are patronymic in origin, meaning they stem from the forename of one's father – with 'Johnson,' for example, indicating 'son of John.'

It was the Normans, in the wake of their eleventh century conquest of Anglo-Saxon England, a pivotal moment in the nation's history, who first brought surnames into usage – although it was a gradual process.

For the Normans, these were names initially based on the title of their estates, local villages and chateaux in France to distinguish and identify these landholdings.

Such grand descriptions also helped enhance the prestige of these warlords and generally glorify their lofty positions high above the humble serfs slaving away below in the pecking order who had only single names, often with Biblical connotations as in Pierre and Jacques.

The only descriptive distinctions among the peasantry concerned their occupations, like 'Pierre the swineherd' or 'Jacques the ferryman.'

Roots of surnames that came into usage in England not only included Norman-French, but also Old French, Old Norse, Old English, Middle English, German, Latin, Greek, Hebrew and the Gaelic languages of the Celts.

The Normans themselves were originally Vikings, or 'Northmen', who raided, colonised and eventually settled down around the French coastline.

The had sailed up the Seine in their longboats in 900AD under their ferocious leader Rollo and ruled the roost in north eastern France before sailing over to conquer England in 1066 under Duke William of Normandy – better known to posterity as William the Conqueror, or King William I of England.

Granted lands in the newly-conquered England, some of their descendants later acquired territories in Wales, Scotland and Ireland – taking not only their own surnames, but also the practice of adopting a surname, with them.

But it was in England where Norman rule and custom first impacted, particularly in relation to the adoption of surnames.

This is reflected in the famous *Domesday Book*, a massive survey of much of England and Wales, ordered by William I, to determine who owned what, what it was worth and therefore how much they were liable to pay in taxes to the voracious Royal Exchequer.

Completed in 1086 and now held in the National Archives in Kew, London, 'Domesday' was an Old English word meaning 'Day of Judgement.'

This was because, in the words of one contemporary chronicler, "its decisions, like those of the Last Judgement, are unalterable."

It had been a requirement of all those English landholders – from the richest to the poorest – that they identify themselves for the purposes of the survey and for future reference by means of a surname.

This is why the *Domesday Book*, although written in Latin as was the practice for several centuries with both civic and ecclesiastical records, is an invaluable source for the early appearance of a wide range of English surnames.

Several of these names were coined in connection with occupations.

These include Baker and Smith, while Cooks, Chamberlains, Constables and Porters were to be found carrying out duties in large medieval households.

The church's influence can be found in names such as Bishop, Friar and Monk while the popular name of Bennett derives from the late fifth to mid-sixth century Saint Benedict, founder of the Benedictine order of monks.

The early medical profession is represented by Barber, while businessmen produced names that include Merchant and Sellers.

Down at the village watermill, the names that cropped up included Millar/Miller, Walker and Fuller, while other self-explanatory trades included Cooper, Tailor, Mason and Wright.

Even the scenery was utilised as in Moor, Hill, Wood and Forrest – while the hunt and the chase supplied names that include Hunter, Falconer, Fowler and Fox.

Colours are also a source of popular surnames, as in Black, Brown, Gray/Grey, Green and White, and would have denoted the colour of the clothing the person habitually wore or, apart from the obvious exception of 'Green', one's hair colouring or even complexion.

The surname Red developed into Reid, while

Blue was rare and no-one wanted to be associated with yellow.

Rather self-important individuals took surnames that include Goodman and Wiseman, while physical attributes crept into surnames such as Small and Little.

Many families proudly boast the heraldic device known as a Coat of Arms, as featured on our front cover.

The central motif of the Coat of Arms would originally have been what was borne on the shield of a warrior to distinguish himself from others on the battlefield.

Not featured on the Coat of Arms, but highlighted on page three, is the family motto and related crest – with the latter frequently different from the central motif.

Adding further variety to the rich cultural heritage that is represented by surnames is the appearance in recent times in lists of the 100 most common names found in England of ones that include Khan, Patel and Singh – names that have proud roots in the vast sub-continent of India.

Echoes of a far distant past can still be found in our surnames and they can be borne with pride in commemoration of our forebears.

Chapter two:

Fields of battle

The Wood name is intriguing in that there are at least four possible sources of derivation.

One is that it derives from the Old English 'wudu', indicating a wood, someone who worked in a wood, or someone who worked with wood, while another source is the Norman-French 'de Vosco', or 'de Bosco', indicating 'wood.'

Another more colourful source of the name is the Anglo-Saxon 'Wod', the name of a feared Germanic god of storm that came to describe someone who became frenzied, or crazed, with the bloodlust of battle – and it is perhaps more than coincidence that the Coat of Arms of at least one branch of the Woods features a crest of a naked savage wielding a club, while the motto is 'Defend.'

'Wood' is the most common form of the name today, with 'Woods' more prevalent in Northern Ireland, with both forms English translations of 'O'Coill', or 'Coil' – names that in turn are derived from the Irish-Gaelic 'coill', indicating a wood.

Bearers of the Wood name, in a number of

early and rather confusing but now defunct variations such as 'Wod', 'Woid', 'Vode' and 'Vould', make their way onto the written record from an early date, but in England they are particularly associated with a family who settled in Leicestershire in the wake of the Norman Conquest of 1066.

By this date, England had become a nation with several powerful competitors to the throne.

In what were extremely complex family, political and military machinations, the monarch was the Anglo-Saxon Harold II, who had succeeded to the throne following the death of Edward the Confessor.

But his right to the throne was contested by two powerful competitors – his brother-in-law King Harold Hardrada of Norway, in alliance with Tostig, Harold II's brother, and Duke William II of Normandy.

In what has become known as The Year of Three Battles, Hardrada invaded England and gained victory over the English king on September 20 at the battle of Fulford, in Yorkshire.

Five days later, however, Harold II decisively defeated his brother-in-law and brother at the battle of Stamford Bridge.

But he had little time to celebrate his victory, having to immediately march south from Yorkshire to encounter a mighty invasion force, led by Duke William of Normandy that had landed at Hastings, in East Sussex.

Harold's battle-hardened but exhausted force of Anglo-Saxon soldiers confronted the Normans on October 14 in a battle subsequently depicted on the Bayeux tapestry – a 23ft. long strip of embroidered linen thought to have been commissioned eleven years after the event by the Norman Odo of Bayeux.

Harold drew up a strong defensive position, at the top of Senlac Hill, building a shield wall to repel Duke William's cavalry and infantry.

The Normans suffered heavy losses, but through a combination of the deadly skill of their archers and the ferocious determination of their cavalry they eventually won the day.

Anglo-Saxon morale had collapsed on the battlefield as word spread through the ranks that Harold had been killed – the Bayeux Tapestry depicting this as having happened when he was struck by an arrow to the head.

Amidst the carnage of the battlefield, it was difficult to identify him – the last of the Anglo-Saxon kings.

Some sources assert William ordered his

body to be thrown into the sea, while others state it was secretly buried at Waltham Abbey.

What is known with certainty, however, is that William in celebration of his great victory founded Battle Abbey, near the site of the battle, ordering that the altar be sited on the spot where Harold was believed to have fallen.

William was declared King of England on December 25, and the complete subjugation of his Anglo-Saxon subjects followed.

Those Normans who had fought on his behalf were rewarded with the lands of Anglo-Saxons.

Among them was the Norman knight Ernald de Bosco – sometimes rendered as de Vosco – and it was his family who came to hold lands in Thorpe Vale, Leicestershire.

It is this family who have the motto of 'The tree may be recognised by its fruits' and crest of an oak tree.

Confusing matters somewhat, it was less than 100 years after the Conquest that the family lost the bulk of its English lands – but found new lands in Scotland after being invited to settle there, along with other Anglo-Normans, by the Scots monarch David II.

Anglicising their name to Wood, they firstly

settled in Dumfriesshire and later acquired further lands much further north in Angus, North Esk and Largo Bay, in Fife.

Recognised as a clan, the proud motto of the Scottish Woods is 'Safe on the waves' and crest a ship under sail.

Ironically, it was a prominent member of this family – who had originally been settled in Leicestershire – who proved a particular thorn in the flesh for England during its frequently turbulent relationships with Scotland.

This was through the Leith-based merchant, sea captain and later High Admiral of Scotland Sir Andrew Wood.

Born in about 1455, he utilised his considerable naval skills under both James III and James IV to protect Scottish vessels from English, Portuguese and Dutch pirates – while also accruing a tidy sum for the Scottish Exchequer by, in turn, preying on them.

Owner of the fighting vessels the *Flower* and the *Yellow Caravel*, one of his most noted naval engagements came in 1490, a number of months after he had captured five English merchant vessels off Dunbar, on Scotland's east coast.

The English retaliated by preparing a heavily

armed fleet that launched an attack on Wood's ships in the Firth of Forth. The battle lasted two days, with crowds lining the shore to watch the engagement.

Despite being outnumbered and outgunned, Wood captured the English vessels – and it was for this that he was knighted by James IV and granted the Barony of Largo where, using captured English seamen, he built a castle overlooking Largo Bay, and of which only a ruined tower now remains.

In later centuries and in many different conflicts, no fewer than four Woods have been honoured with the Victoria Cross (VC), the highest award for gallantry for British and Commonwealth forces.

Born in 1818, John Wood had been a captain in the 20th Bombay Native Infantry, British Indian Army, during the Persian War, when, in December of 1856 at Bushire, Persia (now Iran), he was at the head of an assault column.

The assault was on an enemy fort and Captain Wood was the first to reach the parapet, where he immediately came under attack by the garrison.

Despite being struck by several musket balls, he killed the enemy leader and, followed by his men, overcame the garrison and took the fort.

Wood, who later achieved the rank of Colonel, died in 1878, while his VC was the first to be won in a British Indian Army Regiment.

Born in 1838 near Braintree, in Essex, Field Marshall Sir Henry Wood received his VC for his part in an action in October of 1858 at Sinwaho, during the Indian Mutiny.

Then a lieutenant with the 17th Lancers, he attacked and drove off a band of rebels and later rescued a local merchant whom another band of rebels were about to execute.

The soldier, who also saw action in the Zulu War of 1879, died in 1919 having attained the rank of Field Marshall.

The two other Victoria Crosses awarded to soldiers of the name of Wood were all won during the terrible carnage of the First World War.

Wilfred Wood, born in 1897 and who survived until the age of 85, had been a private in the 10th Battalion, The Northumberland Fusiliers, when in October of 1918, near Casa Vana, Italy, he single-handedly destroyed two enemy machine-gun nests, resulting in the surrender of 300 men.

The other recipient of the VC was Henry Wood, who was born in 1882 in Newton-on-Derwent,

Yorkshire, and who also gained his award in October of 1918.

It was while he was serving as a corporal with the 2nd Battalion, Scots Guards, in St Python, France, that he took command of his platoon after its sergeant was killed and led a successful crossing under heavy fire of a vital river crossing; later promoted to Lance Corporal, he died in 1924.

Chapter three:

Creative minds

Away from the battlefield, bearers of the Wood name have shown a particular flair for invention and business.

One in the field of medicine was the Scottish physician Alexander Wood, born in Edinburgh in 1817 and who died in 1884.

A descendant of Sir Andrew Wood, the Lord High Admiral of Scotland, and a member of the Royal College of Physicians of Edinburgh, he is credited with the invention in 1853 of the first hypodermic needle to use a syringe and hollow needle.

His wife, ironically, was a morphine addict and died from an overdose that she administered into her veins using her husband's revolutionary invention.

Recognised as a pioneer of ultraviolet and infrared photography and its applications, Robert Williams Wood was the American physicist and inventor born in 1868 in Concord, Massachusetts.

Professor of optical physics at John Hopkins University, he developed what is known as Wood's Lamp – the ultraviolet lamp used in medicine – while the Wood Effect describes the glowing appearance of foliage photographed by infrared.

Recipient of honours that include the Henry Draper Medal of the National Academy of Sciences he died in 1955, while the crater Wood on the far side of the Moon is named in his honour.

Born in 1880 in Mapletown, Iowa, Garfield Arthur Wood was the American entrepreneur and inventor better known as Gar Wood.

His many inventions include a hydraulic lift that he first designed to unload coal from railway trucks, while as a boating enthusiast he set a number of world water speed records from 1920 to 1932 for racing a specially adapted motorboat.

His first world record – of 74.870mph – came in 1920 when he raced his motorboat *Miss America* along the Detroit River.

On the St Clair River in 1932, he became the first man to travel at more than 100mph on water, reaching a speed of 124.860mph.

One of his most spectacular stunts had come eleven years earlier when he raced one of his boats against the Havana Special train – a distance of 1,250 miles up the Atlantic coast from Miami to New York City.

Taking a time of 47 hours and 23 minutes, he reached New York twelve minutes ahead of the train.

Having established the Wood Hoist Company in Detroit, later Garwood Industries, he died in 1971.

A pioneer of underwater acoustics and sonar, Albert Beaumont Wood was the British physicist better known as A. B. Wood.

Born in 1890 in Uppermill, Yorkshire, he joined a noted team of fellow scientists at Manchester University who included Sir Ernest Rutherford, Hans Geiger and Neil Bohr.

Appointed a research fellow at Liverpool University when aged 24, in October of 1915 he was appointed to the Board of Invention and Research to explore novel ways of aiding Britain's war effort against Germany.

His efforts led to the gradual development of what became known as sonar, then known as ASDIC (Allied Supreme Detection Investigation Committee) to detect enemy submarines.

Later deputy of the Admiralty Research Laboratory and deputy director of research for the Royal Scientific Service, he was the author of a number of important textbooks that include *A*

Textbook of Sound, first published in 1930 and with a revised edition published in 1955.

The recipient of an OBE in 1939 in recognition of having taken on the highly delicate and dangerous task of dismantling a German mine he died in 1964, while other awards and honours include the Duddell Medal of the Institute of Physics and the Pioneers of Underwater Acoustics Medal from the Acoustical Society of America.

In the world of business, Andrew Trew Wood was the Irish-Canadian businessman and politician born in 1826 in Co. Armagh.

Immigrating to Canada when he was aged about 20, he established his own hardware store in Hamilton ten years later, his wealth eventually allowing him to become a founding director of the Hamilton and Lake Erie Railway Company in 1869 and, in 1881, the Ontario Cotton Mills Company.

Also an owner and first president of the Hamilton Steel and Iron Company, Wood served as a Liberal member of the Canadian House of Commons and, from 1901 until his death two years later, in the Canadian Senate.

In the more contemporary world of business, Sir Ian Wood is the Scots-born businessman whose

Wood Group services not only the North Sea oil industry but also those of more than 50 other countries.

Born in Aberdeen, he served as chief executive of Wood Group from 1967 to 2006 and as its chairman until 2012.

In 2010 he offered £85m to Aberdeen City Council towards a £140m proposed project to redesign his home city's Union Terrace Gardens.

But the proposed redevelopment proved controversial with some local residents and, although later 'passed' by a referendum in the city, it was eventually rejected by the council.

Awarded a CBE in 1982, he was further honoured with a knighthood twelve years later.

In the creative world of architecture, John Wood, known as John Wood the Elder, was the English architect born in Twiverton, near Bath, in 1704, the son of a local builder.

An antiquarian in addition to architect, he extensively surveyed the mysterious Stonehenge megalithic complex in 1740, but he is best known for his landmark architectural work in Bath that includes Queen Square and The Circus.

Described as one of the outstanding architects of the day, he died in 1754.

His son, known as John Wood the Younger, born in 1728 and who died in 1782, followed in his father's visionary footsteps by carrying out famous architectural work in Bath that includes the Royal Crescent and the Bath Assembly Rooms, while he also completed work on the Circus following his father's death.

Chapter four:

On the world stage

To the worlds of film, sport and music, bearers of the Wood and Woods names have stamped their mark at an international level.

Aged only eight when he made his film debut in *Back to the Future Part II*, **Elijah Wood** is the American actor who was born in 1981 in Cedar Rapids, Iowa, and is best known for his role as Frodo Baggins in the 2001-2003 *Lord of the Rings* trilogy of films.

Further international success has followed with films that include the 2004 *Eternal Sunshine of the Spotless Mind* and the 2007 *Day Zero*, while as a voice actor he is the voice of Spyro the Dragon in the video gaming series of that name.

An Academy Award nominee for Best Supporting Actress for her role as Mother Abbess in the 1965 *The Sound of Music*, **Peggy Wood** was the acclaimed American actress of stage, television and film who was born in 1892 in Brooklyn, New York.

The actress, who was also known for her role

from 1949 to 1957 in the American television series *Mama*, died in 1978.

In contemporary times, **James Woods** is the American stage, television and film actor who was born in 1947 in Vernal, Utah, and whose films include the 1973 *The Way We Were*, the 1986 *Salvador*, and, from 1996, *Ghosts of Mississippi*.

The daughter of Russian immigrants to America, **Natalie Wood** was the American actress who was born Natalia Zacharenko in San Francisco in 1938.

Making her film debut as a child actress in the 1943 *Happy Land*, she went on to enjoy further success in films that include the 1955 *Rebel Without A Cause*, starring opposite James Dean, and for which she received an Academy Award nomination for Best Supporting Actress.

Further Academy nominations followed for her performances in the 1961 *Splendor in the Grass* and the 1963 *Love With the Proper Stranger*, while she also won a Golden Globe Award for her role in the 1979 television adaptation of *From Here to Eternity*.

Married to American actor Robert Wagner from 1957 until the couple divorced in 1962, they remarried ten years later.

It was while on a boating trip with her husband and a group of friends near California's Santa Catalina Island in November of 1981 that the actress drowned in mysterious circumstances – giving rise to a number of conspiracy theories that persist to this day.

Her final film, *Brainstorm*, was released two years after her death.

Born in 1919 in Forrest City, Arkansas, **George Wood** was the American film and television actor best known for his role as General Hammond in the television series *M*A*S*H*; he died in 2001.

Also on the stage, George Wood, born in 1894 in Jarrow, South Tyneside was the English actor and comedian better known as **Wee Georgie Wood**.

Only 4ft 9ins in height when fully grown, his career spanned a 50-year period in music hall revues, plays and films; he died in 1979.

Starting her career in 1974 after winning the British television talent show *New Faces*, **Victoria Wood** was the multi-talented actress, singer, comedienne and writer who was born in 1953 in Prestwich, Lancashire.

The recipient in 2005 of the British Comedy Awards' Lifetime Achievement Award, her many other awards include a BAFTA for Best Television Actress for her role in the 2007 *Housewife, 49*, and a British Comedy Awards' Writer of the Year Award in 2001 for her sitcom *dinnerladies*; she died in 2016.

Bearers of the Wood and Woods names have also excelled, and continue to excel, in the highly competitive world of sport.

Born Eldrick Tont Woods in 1975 in Cypress, California, **Tiger Woods** is the American professional golfer rated as one of the most successful players of all time.

Taking up the game at the tender age of only two, at the age of 15 he became the youngest ever U.S. Junior Champion, while, at the time of writing, he has had more than 71 Professional Golf Association (PGA) Tour wins, two Japanese Golf Tour wins, 1 PGA Tour of Australasia win and 15 other professional wins.

Woods, who married the former Swedish model Elin Nordegren in 2004, and with whom he has two children, suffered a blow to his popularity and reputation when it was revealed in 2009 that he had been involved in a number of extra-marital affairs.

Also on the golf course, **Craig Wood** was the American professional golfer who was born in 1901 at Lake Placid, New York. The winner of 21 PGA Tour titles in the 1930s and 1940s and a member of three Ryder Cup teams, the golfer, who died in 1968, was elected to the World Golf Hall of Fame in 2008.

In the sport of curling, **Kelly Wood**, born in Dundee in 1981, was Scottish Junior Curling Champion on no fewer than three occasions, while she is also a three-time winner of the Scottish Women's Championship.

Keeping it in the family, her younger sister, **Lindsay Wood**, was Scottish Women's Champion in both 2005 and 2006.

From curling to bowling, **Willie Wood**, born in 1938 in Haddington, East Lothian is the Scottish professional player who is a recipient of two Commonwealth Games gold medals and two World Bowls Championship runner-up medals.

Also a recipient of an MBE for services to sport, he was inducted into the Scottish Sports Hall of Fame in 2007.

In football, or soccer as it is more commonly known in North America, **Alexander Wood** was the Scots-American defender who was born in 1907 in Lochgelly, Fife.

Moving with his family when aged 12 to Gary, Indiana, he later played for U.S. soccer teams that included the Brooklyn Wanderers, before moving to England in 1933 to play for teams that included Leicester City and Nottingham Forest.

Returning to the U.S. following his retirement from the game in 1939, he was inducted a year before his death in 1987 into America's National Soccer Hall of Fame.

In the much different game of American football, **Barry Wood** was not only a gifted player but also a leading academic in the field of medicine and microbiology.

Born in 1910 in Milton, Massachusetts, he played quarterback for Harvard during the 1929 to 1931 seasons, and later pursued a medical career at both Washington University in St Louis and John Hopkins University; he died in 1971 and was elected to the College Football Hall of Fame in 1980.

The Woods have also produced a number of distinguished historians.

Born in 1865 in Salford, **George Arnold Wood** was the English-Australian historian whose definitive *The Discovery of Australia* was published in 1922, and who held the chair of Challis Professor of History at the University of Sydney until his death in 1928.

In contemporary times, **Michael Wood** is the British historian, broadcaster and documentary filmmaker who was born in 1948 in Manchester.

His books include the 2003 *Shakespeare* and the 2005 *In Search of Myths and Heroes*, while his documentary films include the 1997 *In the Footsteps of Alexander the Great* and, from 2007, *The Story of India*.

In the world of music, **Ronnie Wood** is the English rock guitarist and songwriter best known as a member of the Rolling Stones.

Born in 1947 in Hillingdon, London, the guitarist played with a number of bands, including the Jeff Beck Group and Rod Stewart and the Faces, before becoming a full-time member of the Rolling Stones in 1976.

As a songwriter, he has co-written a number of hit songs that include Rod Stewart's *Gasoline Alley* and the Stones' *Had it With You*.

The recipient in 2009 of an Outstanding Contribution award at the Classic Rock and Roll of Honour ceremony in London, he is also an accomplished artist whose works are frequently exhibited.

A founding member of the English rock band Traffic, **Chris Wood** was the musician born in 1944 in Birmingham and whose album hits with the band include the 1967 *Mr Fantasy*, the 1971 *The Low Spark of High Heeled Boys* and, from 1974, *When the Eagle Flies*; he died in 1983.

Also from Birmingham, **Roy Wood** is the musician, singer, songwriter, producer and arranger who first came to fame as one of the founders of the band The Move. Born in 1946, he was also a member of other bands that include Electric Light Orchestra and Wizzard.

In a different musical genre, **Sir Henry Wood** was the English conductor, born in London in 1869, who is credited with having helped to popularise a vast range of orchestral and classical works.

This was through his involvement with the Proms, which he conducted for close on 50 years.

Named the Henry Wood Promenade Concerts following his death in 1964, the annual event in London is now known as the BBC Proms.

Born in Tasmania in 1849, **John Woods** was the New Zealand schoolteacher and songwriter who composed the music for *God Defend New Zealand*, the country's national anthem.

In the equally creative world of art, **Grant Wood** was the American painter, born in 1891 in Anamosa, Iowa, best known for his paintings of America's rural Midwest – in particular his famous 1930 *American Gothic*.

The artist died in 1942, while the iconic *American Gothic* remains in the proud care of the Art Institute of Chicago.

One particularly intriguing bearer of the Wood name was, strictly speaking, not really a Wood at all.

This was the wartime German diplomat Fritz Kolbe who, as a spy for American Intelligence, was known by the codename of **George Wood**.

Born in Berlin in 1900, he passed Nazi secrets to his American 'handlers' from August of 1943 until the end of the war, when he travelled from Nazi Germany to Berne, in neutral Switzerland, on diplomatic missions.

Described as one of the most important Allied spies of the Second World War, he died in 1971.